CONFIDENCE

THE REAL SECRET OF ATTRACTION

COLETTE LAMUSE

CONFIDENCE: The Real Secret of Attraction

ISBN: 978-1-7346970-0-1

DEDICATION

To Bruce.

No matter where we are in space and time, know this:

you have always been enough.

CONTENTS

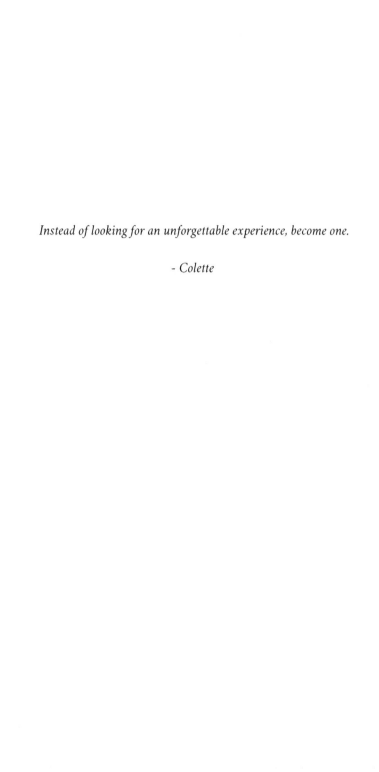

Instead of looking for an unforgettable experience, become one.

- Colette

MEET JOHN

This book is for the man who finds himself in the prime of his life - the have your shit together years - who still feels uncertain and unfulfilled in his romantic relationship(s), and who wants to feel confident and desirable so he can finally attract the stable, loving, and fulfilling life partner he's been searching for.

Like John.

John and Nicole had just finished having sex. No, not the passionate, wild love-making he remembers their relationship starting out with. The only thing raising the temperature in their room these days was the heater. Instead of basking in orgasmic bliss, Nicole headed straight to the bathroom to clean off before returning to bed. Pulling the covers up, she didn't say a word.

John felt the sting of her silence as she turned her back to him, making it clear that she was done for the night. She *was* just doing it to get it done.

Great. Something's wrong, again.

The tension gave way to a familiar spiral of thoughts. John gave in to questioning himself about everything.

Was she disappointed in him again?

For what this time?

Was he that bad in bed?

Did she wish she was with someone else?

Nicole wasn't always easy to read because she would often get quiet and clam up when she was upset. John was well aware of that unsettled feeling, how it silently siphoned the oxygen out of the room.

He ran through the day's events and revisited the past week, the past month. John was keeping score, and he was coming up short.

He *had* fucked up their anniversary date, no surprise to him there. And he wasn't very consistent about taking her out in general, either. Nicole showed less and less interest in him sexually, a sure sign that he was losing ground.

Maybe she'd met someone else? But who? When?

They'd had a few more fights recently, and as usual, he was always "wrong" in the end. Nicole no longer went out of her way to do things for him, make him his favorite food, or show up to bed hungry.

So this is just how it goes...things start off hot and heavy and slowly cool off until they just die out.

What am I missing?

What am I doing wrong?

What am I not doing?

Why does it always seem to go this way?!

It's so easy to make some random woman smile and light up, but I can't seem to cut it with Nicole. She's so distant, like she's already left. I've seen that look before. It won't take long before she does.

Their last fight flashed across his mind.

————

It was nearing 6 pm, his usual arrival time home from work. John took a sharp turn as he instantly remembered their evening plans. Nicole had made all the arrangements for their night out this time. All he had to do was be on time.

Dammit! There I go again...Fucking everything up! She's going to be mad as hell, and I'll never hear the end of it!

Turning into the drive, he decided not to pull into the garage as he usually would. Hoping to slide inconspicuously through their front door, John carefully closed it behind him.

"John? You're late."

Nicole didn't have to say anything else. He knew EXACTLY what she meant. *You're late again. You're such a disappointment. You never get it right. And besides, even if you did, you will **never** make me happy.*

John argued back with the voice in his head. *She's impossible! Everything has to always be her way or the highway.*

The night was a disaster. They were already in a full-blown fight by the time they arrived at the restaurant. On the drive there, Nicole complained to John that he was distracted and not paying attention to her.

"What do you mean I'm not paying attention to you? What are you talking about?! I'm here...in the car...with you. We are going to dinner like you wanted. What am I not doing? Oh, I forgot. You're right. I'm wrong! Why don't I just hurry up and admit it so we can move on... You're never satisfied until you're in control, and you have to control everything! God, Nicole! I should've known this would happen. It always happens."

John audibly exhaled, knowing that letting off that much steam wouldn't make for great conversation, but it was too late. Nicole went completely quiet just as he pulled up to the restaurant.

Great! Now I get the silent treatment. I hate it when she does that! I'm dealing with a fucking child! This is ridiculous.

John felt the thick restaurant air playing tricks on his breathing. Relaxing was nearly impossible. He would have just left but didn't want to deal with *that* aftermath. A few beers in, he started cooling off. Trying to make small talk with Nicole to round out the awkward edge didn't do him any good. She wasn't going to speak. Not a damn word.

When they had finished eating, she got up first, making sure to walk a few steps ahead of him. Pushing the restaurant door open for herself, she stood off to the side while they waited for valet.

John pulled into the garage and turned the car off, punching the steering wheel. *Hard.*

"This is bullshit. I work my ass off for this?!"

John knew Nicole would head straight to the bedroom, so he didn't. Instead, he found his way to the living room couch and started flipping the channels until an old action movie turned up. He could care less that he'd seen it before. The stress of the day had finally won, and he was out.

————

During our initial session, John confided to me that he was nearing the "fuck it" point. He felt like all they ever did was fight. There wasn't even any make up sex. He was "over" the public embarrassment. Truth be told, John was tired. Tired of feeling like a disappointment. Tired of feeling frustrated. Tired of being confused. Tired of never making Nicole happy.

John admitted that he wasn't afraid of commitment, as Nicole had often thought, but he hated feeling controlled. Or was it *out of* control?

Deep down, he didn't really feel fulfilled in this relationship, or his last few, for that matter. He couldn't quite put his finger on it, but he knew that certain something was missing, that something that would reassure him that this was *the* relationship worth fighting for. He wanted to be sure before he fully committed to a woman.

John openly shared that most of his frustration with Nicole was actually more of a frustration with himself, with life. He hated feeling stuck, confused, and...*lonely*. He was on the right track.

When John felt this frustration, disappointment, and confusion, he got angry. Some men isolate themselves, get quiet, and withdraw. Still others will try even harder to please or appease the woman. Often it's a combination.

What about you?

Are you frustrated?

Have your relationships (or lack of) left you feeling uncertain and unfulfilled? *Alone?*

Do you feel like you're starting back at square one, wondering what's wrong with you?

Perhaps you've even had your silent or not so silent "fuck this shit" moment...

Having chosen to read this book, I know you are looking for a real solution. You may have even tried some other proposed solutions, only to end up still dealing with the same frustrating cycle all over again.

This unwanted pattern can end once and for all.

Speaking of frustrating cycles, do you ever get caught in the following sequence: See problem. Attempt solution. Solution doesn't work or worked only temporarily. Back at problem *again*.

This is usually because the proposed solution was focusing on going after the symptom(s) rather than the cause. The root feeds the fruit.

The key to finally ending this frustrating relationship pattern requires you to own and shift out of a chief operating belief.

The belief: **I am not enough.**

This book will uncover the five main areas where this belief is in covert operation and the most common ways it shows up in a man's life, silently sabotaging his relationships.

Listen. Some people hold out the answer, the *secret*, until the end of a book or tuck it away in something else you need to buy. I love you too much to hide anything from you, especially a truth that will completely change your life. I'm going to give you the answer right now.

The answer: Only believe.

"Believe *what*?!" You ask? That you, my love, **are** what/who you **desire to be**.

In this book, I will highlight two types of men:

1. The man with the core operating belief: **I am not enough**, and
2. The man who believes **I AM enough**

You will clearly see the difference for yourself and decide who you will be moving forward.

I'm not hiding the answer to attracting the woman you desire, either. Confidence - true confidence - is the ONE thing you need to attract the woman of your dreams and to keep her satisfied.

Confidence **IS** the core operating belief: **I AM (enough)** to be and thus have all I desire.

There is no other hidden secret to success. This is the ONE thing you need to succeed in *all* areas of life. True confidence doesn't necessarily look like what you've been taught or what you have seen with other men who appear to be confident or to have it all together.

This duality can be frustrating or confusing, which is why I have chosen to lay it out in a very straightforward manner, so you can see it for yourself, in black and white.

Now, at the back of this book, there are resources for you to access me, my teachings, and the gift I have to facilitate transformation in men - radical transformation through remembering who you have always already been, reconnecting to your true innate confidence and identity found within your own heart/soul.

As I stated, the answer - **the secret** - is that you are already enough and that by believing and operating from that core belief, everything will change.

EVERYTHING WILL CHANGE.

The problem is deep down you don't believe you are enough, not yet, anyway.

You may or may not be aware of this contradiction between your conscious and subconscious mind. But know this - your subconscious thoughts are governing your life. What you are experiencing, frustrating cycles and all, are tethered to the subconscious belief **I am not enough**.

My work and resources are here to facilitate your internal shift to **I AM enough**.

And you *so* are.

The problem is not that you are not enough.

The problem is that you don't know you already are.

- Colette

IT'S YOUR DECISION

A s I stated earlier, this book is for the man who finds himself in the prime of his life - the have your shit together years - **who still feels uncertain and unfulfilled in his romantic relationship(s), and who wants to feel confident and desirable** so he can finally attract the stable, loving and fulfilling life partner he's been searching for.

Listen. You will not and cannot attract your *ideal* partner as long as you have the deep core belief **I am not enough**. Now let me be clear - I'm not saying you can't or won't attract *a* partner...she just won't be your ideal partner because we always attract on our level of confidence. In other words, your level of confidence (or insecurity), is the level you can attract in a woman.

If you are finally done with feeling uncertain and unfulfilled in your relationships, and you are ready to do whatever it takes to attract your ideal life partner, then this is your non-negotiable first step:

You must decide to step into your *enoughness*.

To do this, you must first be willing to look at your current core operating belief and how it shows up in your life. In the chapters to come, we will be looking at the difference between being enough and not being enough and some of the common ways this shows up in key areas of your life. Seeing those examples will help you connect the dots back to your own specific thoughts, feelings, and actions.

After that, it comes down to a basic two-step process:

1. **Own your shit.**
2. **Shift your shit.**

It's time for you to un-fuck with the bullshit.

Are you ready?

If so, keep reading. Let's do the damn thing.

If not, you might as well not read this book because none of this will work if you don't work it.

But I know you know how to work it. I'll see you on the inside. xxoo.

It's so much better when we come together.

- Colette

COME WITH ME

S o you decided to take the ride. I like your boldness, your courage.

From now on, this book assumes the position that you are ready to face off with the core belief **I am not enough** and that you will begin to own the belief **I AM enough**, as you learn to shift every limiting thought, belief, or feeling that tells you otherwise.

Before we shine a spotlight on the five main areas where this core belief is in full-blown covert operation, let's look at being *enough*.

The phrase "being enough" doesn't necessarily imply being perfect or having to be the best, but it does indicate an analysis of some sort.

There isn't an exact science that measures one's enoughness, but it is commonly believed that we are either "enough," "not enough," or "almost enough" (which we know really means we are not enough).

"Being enough" is an expressed state of identity.

**The truth of the matter is you ARE enough.
The problem is you haven't fully believed it.**

When we identify in the core of our being that we are enough, then what we do comes *from* this enoughness. Conversely, when we identify as not being enough, what we do is in order to attain or validate our enoughness. And in some cases, it is even how we bring evidence against our enoughness and thereby strengthen our belief that we are not enough.

What you do is not as important as *why* you do what you do. Your actions are not as telling as the thoughts that drive them. Being enough simply means you are worthy of, good enough for, able to, or allowed to have that which you desire.

We are about to go on a journey together through the five main areas, all of which directly affect your ability to find, attract and keep your ideal life partner. Together, we will uncover that the belief **I am not enough** has been the undercurrent of your life. We will also see the ways you've been masking it and how it has been silently working against your relationships. This discovery will change your life if you allow it.

**The five main areas are:
Relational, Financial, Spiritual, Physical, Sexual**

You may spot one (or more) right away that is a problem area, or perhaps that is not an area of concern for you. However, your core belief operates without partiality. If one of the chapters is an area you feel "good enough" in, I ask that you read the chapter with openness - there may be something to be seen that you haven't previously considered. It is often the case that when a man with the core belief **I am not enough** feels "good enough" in one of these areas, it's because he has learned how to operate more competently than others (by comparison).

If one were to remove all of the building blocks he used to create success in that area, it would expose the weak foundation. To be fully confident and assured in who you are, you must have an immovable, unshakable foundation (identity). Therefore, true confidence cannot be because of anything that can be altered, or else it is unstable and uncertain. This means it cannot be because of appearance, abilities, accomplishments, acquisitions, position, or possessions...

In many instances, when there is a predominant area of perceived lack (feeling not good enough), it is common to excel in another area. This drive is often an overcompensation fueled by the lack. In this case, the actions taken to achieve enoughness here would need to be continually performed in order to maintain the achieved status. Enter THE RAT RACE.

When you shift your core belief to **I AM enough**, it will uplevel you in every single area, bringing balance and stability, without exclusion. Instead of being driven by a sense of lack, you will be motivated with newfound abundance and vigor. Along with knowing you are enough comes the knowledge that you are fully resourced with everything you need to excel in life.

Are you ready, love?

Come with me.

If you want to attract the woman of your dreams,

become the man of yours.

- Colette

4

RELATIONAL

This book is obviously going to touch on relationships, and you're clearly interested in overcoming an undesirable relationship pattern, so it would be naughty of me to make you wait until the end of the book to talk about *this* main area.

To be human is to be relational.

It's to be affected and shaped by the relationships we have, have had, or don't have in our lives.

Relationships are simply the way in which two or more people, concepts, or things are connected, or said another way:

Relationship is the state of being connected.

Before you had an intentional romantic relationship with a woman, you had prior relationships with other men and women (platonic/romantic). These relationships helped to form the majority of your current BS BS (bullshit belief system).

Before we get to females, specifically in the romantic capacity, let's briefly touch on these other relationships and see how the belief **I am not enough** shows up within them.

When a man has the core operating belief **I am not enough** it will affect the feedback loop of the following relationships: Father Figures, Friends, Followers, and Females (maternal/platonic).

Author's Note: Just as I mentioned that not every area in this book will be a flashing light of insecurity, it is the same for the following subareas. I trust that you will see what you need to see and hear what you need to hear. Additionally, this book is not exhaustive or comprehensive in each listed area, as that would be overkill. Rather, I will give you an overview of each of the areas and subareas. In other words, there is more to the story.

Father Figures

Father figures are not limited to those who raised you or who biologically participated in your creation. They are men who stood in a position of leadership in your life. This is any male from childhood until now that you looked up to, learned from, or were led by. It isn't that they necessarily held a position of authority over you or that you even liked them, but that you viewed them, consciously or subconsciously, as an influencer in your personal or professional life. You will have more than one, and there will likely be a pattern within each of your father figure relationships.

Father figures (FF) are not necessarily relationships you enjoyed or wanted, although they could be, and hopefully, they were.

But more often than not, the belief that **I am not enough** is tethered in one way or another to the FF relationships you had that left you feeling less than as a man. The idea of FF also encompasses idealized or imagined/desired relationships. Your idealized FF relationship will reveal a lot about what you feel you are missing or have been missing in your actual relationships.

Many men have suffered the loss of/lack of meaningful, significant FFs and have settled for ones that didn't truly satisfy them, or for FFs they could never fully appease.

When you consider your FFs, you may recall your biological father, an adopted or step-father, an absent father, a friend's father, or other stand-in father, family members (uncle, grandfather, cousin, older brother...), bosses or other leaders in your community, such as pastors, coaches, teachers, or mentors.

When a man's core operational belief is I am not enough, he will have had certain patterned responses to his Father Figures (FF). These responses often pendulate between the following:

- Wants to please FF and make him proud/Doesn't think he does
- Wants to be accepted by FF/Doesn't think he is
- Wants to be led by FF/Doesn't think FF wants to, has the time, or makes the time for him
- Does what he thinks will make FF happy/Avoids what he thinks will make FF unhappy
- Thinks he is wanted by FF/Thinks he is unwanted
- Thinks he is important to FF/Thinks he is unimportant
- Thinks FF is proud of him/Thinks FF is ashamed of

him or that he is not good enough to be shown off
by FF

**When a man doesn't believe he is good enough, he will
also be familiar with the following:**

- Strives to outshine the other men who look up to this
  same FF
- Never seems to fully arrive at being pleasing,
  accepted, or making FF proud, as there is always
  another opportunity, event, situation, game, etc. in
  which he is being tested
- Feels he is always on the cusp of acceptance and
  being taken under FF's wing
- Realizes he is not "in" the FF's true inner circle, but
  still on the larger outer-inner circle
- Feels *less than* some of the other men (brothers) who
  look up to this FF
- Feels *better than* some of the other brothers
- Looks at and analyzes what others are doing to make
  this FF proud/happy and works harder at those things
- Is in a continual cycle of striving and performing in
  order to be loved, wanted, and accepted by his FF,
  but deep down never has full assurance that he is

Friends

When a man has the core belief **I am not enough**, he won't
be able to share his deepest secrets with his friends, even
those he considers to be close friends. His close friends are
often the "better than the others" scenario. And many of the
friends he has fall into the "friends" category. Every man
knows the difference intrinsically.

Even if a man can draw an entire crowd around him, it doesn't mean he can let them in.

A man knows whether he truly has a best friend, someone he can share anything and everything with, without fearing the loss of respect or the friendship itself. A friend like that is a friend indeed.

When a man hasn't had stable, loving, and compassionate father figures, its effects will show up in his interaction with his peers. In many cases, men with this experience will turn everything into a covert competition. The score is always being kept and is continuously being measured against himself.

The area of friendship can be harder to see for some men because they have become very skilled at showing up in friendships in just the right way so as to always be admired and accepted.

Men who have the core belief I am not enough can relate to many of the following thoughts, feelings, and actions when it comes to friendship:

- Avoids revealing or doing the things that would cause a loss of admiration or respect among his friends
- Strives to be seen as a leader among his circle of friends
- Secretly feels not wanted by the "in crowd"/elite group of men that he wants to be wanted by (being wanted by them means he is even more admirable as a man)
- Feels always just outside of being in
- Perhaps even feels he was never really wanted as a

best friend, that no other male peer craves his friendship

- If he gets into the elite group that he wants to be wanted by or be good enough for, then he secretly feels like an impostor, but he strives to make sure no one can see that
- Has come to accept the lack of depth in his friendships
- Doesn't feel deeply satisfied in his friendships; knows there is more that could be had and is keenly aware that he doesn't have it
- Has seen a lot/knows too much, causing him to think that most men cannot be trusted
- Experiences a lot of transactional friends who come to him when they need or want something, but not to be with him for who he is
- Thinks his friends would have less respect or admiration for him if they knew everything about him, or worse, would reject him altogether

Followers

The term *followers* represents the relationship a man has with anyone whom he considers himself to be in leadership or authority over. This can be actual or perceived, physical or spiritual. It is when he sees himself as the teacher or elder in the relationship.

Followers are like sons and daughters, encompassing those you feel responsible for in some way. Although not necessarily male, I will use male descriptors for simplicity.

Your followers are:

Those you father/have fathered, such as: sons, step-sons, younger extended family members, neighborhood kids, a son's friend, even fathers who never got their shit together and who you feel you have "grown beyond"...

Those you lead as a boss, teacher, coach, mentor, pastor, or any position in which you are considered the authority...

Those you influence, such as peers who look up to you, people who admire your work, even your actual followers on social media platforms...

When a man has the core belief I am not enough, he will have certain feelings, thoughts, and actions when it comes to his followers, much like these:

- Expects too much from them; drives them towards perfection
- Pretends he doesn't care what they think
- Cares too much about what they think
- Leads/teaches them in areas and concepts he secretly knows he is struggling with, but doesn't let them know this because he feels ashamed
- Interprets their results as a reflection of how good he is or is not as a leader and, thus, as a man
- Calls out areas they are failing to measure up in, and tells them what they should do about it (meanwhile he can't seem to overcome that same area of struggle)
- Tries harder to get them to be better in their personal or professional lives then they may want to be or are willing to be
- Gets upset if they go against his advice/instruction because it subtly implies that he/his teaching wasn't what they wanted or good enough for them
- Tries harder to be pleasing, to be what 'the people'

want, to be what will make him seen, known, and admired
- Leads others while seeing himself as better than them or thinks he knows more than them
- Leads others while secretly fearing they will discover he is no better than them or that they know more than him
- Is quick to find fault with those who resemble him, his work, or his position
- Questions his followers' loyalty and love
- Always thinks about and plans the next thing, the next move, the next evolution required to remain on top (because anything less than the best = worthless)

Females

Ahh *females*. (sigh)

You've seen a lot when it comes to women - the good, the bad, and the downright ugly. You've seen the hardened, the docile, and the sleazy. And now you're here, wanting something more, someone deeply satisfying, safe, and secure.

Yes, women *can* be unsafe creatures. Have you experienced your fair share of them? Insecure, clingy, demanding, superficial... crazy even...

You want a relationship that is deeply meaningful, delightful and intriguing, and you're tired of being in the scripted one - the one you can predict to a T. You're bored with women who seem to have no personal sense of wonder, purpose, or the deep well of joyful living. I know you desire to be in a relationship with a woman who knows who she is.

Shall I describe her?

She's a woman who's sexy, confident, and chilled the fuck out. She's adventurous, spontaneous, and a little wild at times. Her eyes are full of light and she sees straight through you, arresting your heart as if she's always known you. She's safe, loyal, and authentic AF. She gets you because she takes the time to get to know you.

She loves you because she is radically in love with herself - not to get something from you, especially not her identity, her confidence, her value, or her purpose.

She is kind, yet she is bold. She is loving, yet stands up for who she is and what she believes in. She knows when to lead her life and when to let you lead her. She is beautiful inside and out. She possesses and is possessed by a radiance only your soul can fully comprehend. She is free and nonjudgmental. She sees the good in others while maintaining healthy relational boundaries.

She understands how to enter into the secret place with you, where the two of you know one another and are known without fear or reservation. She accepts you as you are, while always seeing the incredible man you are becoming. She is your biggest fan and your truest friend. The wonder she brings has no end. She delights in you - body, mind, heart, and soul.

She feels like **home**. Mmmm.

Can you see her? Can you feel her?

She's the full package. AND -

She's out there. I promise you.

Keep that picture in your head.

Hold it in your heart.

See her in your arms, your home, your bed.

She's why you're here, reading this book. (At least, you thought that was why you were here.)

Listen, babe. To get to her, we have to first get to *you* - the **you** that is more than enough to attract and keep that gorgeous, smoking hot woman.

Before you can have the woman of your dreams, you must become the man of hers.

She desires a man who is:

Safe

Attractive

Secure

Authentic

Stable

Supportive

Loving

Confident

Bold

Non-judgmental

Honest

Accepting

Integrous

Trustworthy

Inspired

Discerning

Consistent

Relaxed

Protective

Adventurous

Brave

Gentle (and knows when to be rough)

A visionary and a leader (who isn't afraid to let her take the lead in her own life)

Did you notice anything about that list? Weren't those qualities familiar to you? It sounds like you both want the same things in **you**...So,

In order to become the man of her dreams, you must first become the man of *yours*.

No, not the man of your father figures' dreams or the one who your friends admire, or the one who your followers demand - you must become the man YOU have always wanted to be.

Do you see **him**? Good.

Hold that thought. Hold it tight.

Bring it in deep, all the way into your chest.

See him (the REAL you).

Now see **him** with **her**.

Hold that thought - tight and deep... ... ...

Hi. I hate to interrupt that glorious moment of ecstasy, but it's my job to help you see what you need to see in order to believe what you need to believe, so that you can have what you want to have...a lot of it. Yes, gorgeous, I know.

We are taking a hard left here, so I'm giving you a moment to shift with me to another female relationship.

————

THIS IS YOUR MOMENT TO SHIFT

————

You've been in a relationship with a female since the womb. (I told you this was a hard image shift!) Yes, I'm talking about your mother (or mother figure). You may have good memories and feelings about her, or you may have unpleasant ones. Or, perhaps she was absent, and you've had to live without that relationship.

We don't need to over-psychoanalyze your past to get you where you need to be. And once again, it is to be: **enough**. That is what attracts and keeps the woman you desire. But, we do need to lean into the relationships you have had or are having with women so that we can pick up on the underlying patterns that expose the core belief **I am not enough**.

Remember: The belief **I am not enough** is what is keeping you from attracting the woman you desire and **the whole point of this book is to reveal *that*** to you in five main areas,

so that you can see what you need to see in order to shift what you need to shift.

Whether it's your mother/mother figure, other female family members, work acquaintances, business partners, or clients, flirtatious encounters with a stranger that you never intended to go anywhere beyond the moment, a one-night stand, steady girlfriend, or even your wife...Females show up in your life in both dramatic and subtle roles. But it's how *you* interact with them reveals what you really think about yourself and what you do to ensure they think highly of you.

A man who has the core belief I am not enough will respond to women with many of the following feelings, thoughts, and actions:

- Worries about choosing the wrong woman
- Longs to be seen with a gorgeous woman
- Longs to wanted by a gorgeous woman
- Gets nervous around the gorgeous woman he wants to want him
- Thinks he never does the right things around her
- Works hard to get the girl (does all the right things, makes all the right moves, wears the right clothes, cologne, buys the right gift, takes her to the right place, says all the right things, pleasures her in just the right way…)
- Can't figure out why in the world everything he did was right in the beginning and now everything he does is wrong!!!
- Thinks he never does enough for her
- Wonders why women are so much easier (no, not that kind of easy...I'm talking to handle, be with, get along with) *before* the girlfriend phase, and especially

before the wife phase (He dreads the idea of having a second mother.)

- Speaking of his mother, he feels obligated to please her, overly concerned about her, overwhelmed by her, resents her, or simply avoids her altogether
- Wonders if he chose the right woman; questions whether or not this relationship will last; doubts she is "the one"
- Can't stand when she is upset or unhappy and does whatever it takes to fix it (or make it go away)
- Gets quiet/loud/angry when she nags
- Gets the fuck out when she nags
- Wonders why it is so easy to please other women, especially those he just met
- Allows a woman to mistreat him
- Demands a woman respect him
- Fears her reactions and tries to keep her happy
- Avoids or hides things that make her unhappy
- Worries she will leave him; tries to prevent it
- Thinks she is the ONLY one who will love him or who he wants to love, but fears she will leave and that he will be alone in his love for her
- Waits for her to change her mind even though she said she doesn't want to be with him
- Enjoys the release and the rush of getting a female stranger to smile, laugh, or flirt with him
- Enjoys the excitement of watching women lean in, oblige, or make exceptions for him the moment he turns on his charm and suave mannerisms
- Thinks his charm and mannerisms are what it is to be a gentleman and are what women want from him (It works, so it must be, right?)
- Ghosts the woman who has turned out to be too needy or too clingy or too anything

- Is always looking for the better woman/match
- Worries his girlfriend/wife is losing interest in him
- Thinks he is losing interest in her (She is definitely not who he thought she was!)
- Feels frustrated at this whole finding a life partner who is **actually** enjoyable for life
- Wonders why relationships have to be so complicated, stressful, difficult, or boring
- Thinks it is easier to just date the hot chick who doesn't demand anything from him
- Knows "the hot chick who doesn't demand anything from him" would bore his brains out, and that after a certain amount of her driving him crazy in bed, she would drive him crazy in the head because she could never get deep enough to reach in and touch who he really is
- Thinks if he can **relationally** please or impress, he will attract the woman of his dreams and keep her satisfied

Remember John? When he first met Nicole, she was head over heels for him. She couldn't get enough of him in bed, or otherwise. Boy! Did she have the hots for him, until she grew cold that is. He was confused by her change in temperature and couldn't figure out if it was him or her or both - or WTF it was. But he knew this thing was not what he thought it was. And he knew it wouldn't last if it didn't change (back) soon.

John had tried everything. Honestly, he had. He was a well-meaning, all-around good guy. He was loyal, for the most part, although he did admit to dabbling in a little porn here and there or checking out an attractive woman. "What guy doesn't?" He asked, clearly not expecting an answer from me.

That last argument and subsequent downhill slide of their sex life was what led him to seek me out. He had really thought Nicole was going to be "the one." Now he wasn't so sure, and he was tired of ending up back at those damned familiar feelings: **uncertain and unfulfilled**.

He wanted to know what he was missing. As much as he felt like she was the problem, deep down, he wasn't sure it was all on her. And if there was anything for him to own, he wanted me to give it to him straight. So I did, *professionally*, that is.

Some do like it rough, you know...

When a man's core belief is I AM enough. He will think, feel, and act in very specific ways. He will approach romantic relationships, much like the following:

- He is not constantly searching for a woman who finds him attractive, desirable, or who wants him
- He is looking for a good-looking woman, but doesn't need her to make him look good
- He is creating the life of his dreams, the life he envisions when he gets out bed every day
- He knows that the woman he desires is a match for him in every way and they can't help but meet
- He knows that when she comes into his world, he will be the man of hers - not because of what he can do for her or provide for her, but because of WHO HE IS
- He knows that he is good enough in life, in business, and in bed
- He is not looking for women to validate him, acknowledge, or appreciate him, yet they do
- He is confident and suave - not to get anything from

a woman, but because he feels at ease in his own innate masculine flow and he wants to share it with her

- He is aware of areas he wants to improve and/or personal struggles, but he doesn't beat himself up or get down on himself because of them
- He does the inner work necessary to fulfill and fully embody the man he knows he is inside
- He enjoys himself and women enjoy his presence
- He doesn't settle for cheap thrills; if any man can have her, he doesn't want her
- He knows he is worthy of any woman he desires
- He believes he can have the woman of his dreams
- He isn't scrambling, trying too hard, or over-analyzing his every move
- He is relaxed, sure of himself and well put together - not merely on the outside, but because his inner world is at rest
- He shows up as himself, attractive AF and this magnetizes the woman he desires
- He is stable and secure in his ability to provide
- He knows a woman can never be rescued from her own emotional disposition of lack and doesn't play the savior role
- He is loving and generous AF
- He doesn't hold back who he is, set aside things that are important to him, or stop showing up confident in life because of a woman
- He has no secrets that he is too afraid to share with the woman he wants to share a life with
- He sees the woman inside, past the smoking hot body for who she really is, and decides based off of *her* if she is what he really wants in a life partner
- He doesn't spend his time, money, or energy

pursuing a woman unless she shows signs of potential and **he knows exactly what those signs are**

- He stops pursuing a woman when it becomes obvious she isn't truly the woman he desires
- He keeps no side chicks, backup chicks, or feeling kinda lonely chicks
- **He knows and embodies the power of true confidence - the ONE thing needed to attract the woman of his dreams and keep her satisfied**

XXOO

A man of worth sees the pearl and buys the whole damn field.

A man who knows nothing of worth sells the fucking field.

- Colette

5

FINANCIAL

The term *finances* refers to more than simply what you make. It encompasses all you possess and receive, which creates the resources that provide for you and allow you to provide for others.

Finances are an ebb and flow of more than simply the material. Remember the definition of **relationship**? It's the way in which two or more people, concepts or things are connected, or said another way: the state of being connected.

How you interact with your finances, your views/beliefs, choices/responses, and how you feel about your finances are all very much consistent with being in a relationship. And your relationship with your finances affects your relationship with females, but of course you already know this.

Finances are a major player when it comes to your movement in life, especially when it comes to how you desire to show up in a relationship with a woman.

The idea of financial abundance elicits images and feelings of freedom, expansion, influence, and enjoying life more fully.

And just as finances can feel freeing, the lack of financial flow can feel restraining, limiting, or even life-threatening.

When you don't feel like you can financially move about freely and powerfully or when you cannot provide the way you want to in your romantic relationship, the topic of finances can elicit frustration or fear.

When you are not secure in your finances, your *financial enoughness*, it will show up in your relationships, silently sabotaging your financial expression and diffusing into the relationship itself.

I'm not one to discount the place of finances.

Having more money is essential to your expansion in this world and it significantly affects all areas of your life, rightfully so.

The more you have, the more you can **do**.

The more you have, the more you can **give**.

The more you have, the more you can **influence** through your **impact**.

Don't buy the BS story that one ought to be "humble," and by humble, they mean "poor" as a means of being good or spiritual. Finances allow you to DO good in addition to simply being good.

Listen, I already know you are a good man. You have a good heart, and you are by nature giving and generous. I know you want to influence those around you. So it's noble to desire more money and a greater, more stable financial foundation on which to build.

Having increase and abundance allows you to release more

of what's in your heart toward the people and projects that matter to you.

Relationally speaking, something as simple as being able to buy the woman of your dreams a ring to signify the depth of your love for her is a beautiful expression of your goodness and generosity. Let alone desiring to provide a home where she can feel safe and secure or the provision for her to follow her dreams. These are no less good than desiring to give generously to major, large-scale causes.

Whatever is in your heart to do matters because it matters to you and because **you matter**.

As major as this topic is, graciously allow me to simplify your relationship with finances to two concepts:

Finances are a mirror and a magnet.

Like a mirror, your finances show you what you believe about yourself and the world you live in. Like a magnet, they are drawn to you and/or repelled away from you by these beliefs. The core of which is either **I am/am not enough**.

If a man believes he is not enough, you can bet your bottom dollar it will show up in his finances.

Now, it is not as cut and dry as a man who believes he is enough will have a lot and a man who doesn't believe he is enough will have only a little. Clearly, you've seen examples on both ends of the spectrum that contradict this oversimplified way of thinking.

A man who operates from the core belief, I am not enough will experience many of the following feelings, thoughts, and actions around finances:

- Feels driven, but not from a place of peace (not from an inspired or relaxed soul)
- Has an underlying thought process to the effect of: **If I provide, I am sufficient. If I don't, I am not.**
- Thinks his survival is dependent on his ability to provide and he is, therefore, driven to survive
- Feels pressured to keep the next thing coming in order to know things are "okay" financially
- Feels like himself, like a *man*, when money is flowing
- Feels undone, ashamed, and incapable when money isn't flowing
- Worries about finances, the future, and being able to provide; fears something bad might happen that will wipe out his finances
- Worries about maintaining his health, fearing its loss could mean he can no longer provide
- Wonders if what he is doing in life (his job/career) is good enough or man enough
- Feels ashamed of his work or work history
- Feels directly tied to what he has accomplished financially and gets his sense of worth from it
- Feels ashamed of his current, past, or potential future financial status
- Wishes he had it easier and that making money wasn't so draining
- Keeps financial score, always knows where he stands financially compared to others around him
- Is silently relieved when others fail financially because it means he's winning or sitting in a higher position (Phew! I'm not *that* bad.)
- Gets his identity from his work or income (whether positively or negatively)
- Believes his ability to make money and to have money gives him value in the eyes of others

- Wonders if his ability to provide will be enough to attract the woman he desires and enough to keep her
- Feels the pressure to outdo other men provisionally
- Feels ashamed if other men are better at it
- Tries even harder to give the woman he wants *everything* that will make her happy
- Fears she may leave if he cannot provide the lifestyle she wants
- Fears that a man with more money can whisk her away
- Fears others will think less of him if they knew his true financial situation
- Makes sure to always appear on top of his finances, even if he is privately drowning
- Gets angry, especially about non-related issues, when he is really afraid about his finances
- Makes financial decisions based on what he lacks, out of fear of loss, or resistance to decrease
- Tries to hide or run from his silent fears; **hiding** can look like not being forthcoming in order to buy time to fix financial discrepancies or to avert financial disaster; **running** can look like distracting his thoughts by keeping busy doing things that don't really matter to him but give him an emotional escape
- Has no desire to leave the security of the financial comfort zone he has achieved, even if it's unfulfilling
- Is only comfortable in chaos and always goes for the gusto, taking substantial risks with reckless abandonment, even at the expense of financial security and stability
- Fears financial failure
- Is embarrassed about his living situation/home, car/transportation, other possessions, or lack thereof

- Blames himself for any perceived failures
- Is driven to avoid financial failure; he plans everything out perfectly to ensure financial success, is overly organized and calculated in his finances, accounting for every last dime
- Thinks if he can **financially** please or impress, he will attract the woman of his dreams and keep her satisfied

Men who have the core belief **I am not enough** may have drastic differences in their financial status. It is more about the thoughts that drive their actions than their achieved position.

Many men have acquired a lot of money driven by the fear of failure. Although outwardly successful, they are anxious inside, meticulously controlling their finances in order to avoid future fallout.

This outcome-focused navigation will show up in their love life, too. They will be very strategic, looking for evidence that ensures success before moving forward to prevent a potential relationship failure. If they are unsure about the viability of a relationship (because they are motivated by fear of it not working out), they will be looking for clues and suspicious activity that indicates that she is not really *all in*.

They want to see **evidence** that the woman is committed to them wholeheartedly before they feel safe to fully invest their heart and finances into the relationship. Calculated risk.

Other men seem to have it easy when it comes to finances, and they don't struggle with fear or lack in this area because they were raised to believe it was safe to make money - lots of it - to take risks and to make financial mistakes.

The core belief **I am not enough** does not always show up in obvious ways, but it will always give evidence to its existence. A man who can't seem to spot it directly in a major area like finances still knows its presence when he is alone with himself.

Other men may work hard, but struggle to make a decent living, wishing they had done things differently or had taken a different route in life. They wish they could somehow get ahead or catch a break, but feel like life just doesn't favor them the way it does other men.

Some men make a comfortable living, but still feel unfulfilled financially because they don't believe their work is significant, or it's not what they would be doing if they could do what they really want to do, knowing they would succeed at it.

———

John understood the financial struggle well. He wanted to be a good provider. He wanted to come out on top at work, in life and at home with Nicole. He wanted people to see him as a success and to be proud of him. He wanted to be admired.

When he was winning, he *was* those things. When he was losing, he felt dispensable, replaceable. Nicole never said it directly, but he saw her frustration. She wanted to be able to "do other things," follow her "dreams," but he couldn't always afford to make it happen for her.

They'd been together for a couple of years, and he often thought about buying her a ring, but he couldn't afford the ring he felt she deserved. Deep down, the ring was a reflection of his ability to provide. It was a measure of his man factor, and he was ashamed at the thought of it being small.

Small when it comes to men is often the degrading "s" word. No man wants to hear he is small, or what he has is small, or what he does is small. And certainly, no man wants to have a small you know...but we will talk more about that when we get to the chapter on sexuality.

When things weren't going well at work, frustration and anger would rise up to hide his underlying fear.

What if she sees that I'm failing and thinks I'm not a real man, or that another man could provide better for her or give her the life she wants?

He wanted her to have it. He just didn't know if he was going to be able to give it to her fast enough. Sometimes his frustration with himself would boil over into an argument with Nicole where he would end up accusing her, saying things like:

You never appreciate what I do.

It's never good enough for you.

You're always looking for a reason to leave.

But John knew deep down those were *his* fears.

When a man's core belief is I AM enough, his relationship to finances will look, and feel more like the following:

- He is unattached to the outcomes, trusting that everything is always working itself out for him
- He is not defined by his financial status
- He doesn't feel the need to hide; feels no shame
- He is honest and open when it comes to discussing his finances within his romantic relationship
- He is generous and gives as his heart/soul prompts him to

- He always sees himself as a financial provider for his woman, to ease and better her existence
- He enjoys giving to the one he loves out of the abundance of the love he has for her
- He is able to recognize and is not attracted to a woman who is desperate for his provision
- He is able to recognize and is not attracted to a woman who is attracted to him for his financial status or what he can give to/buy for her
- He does not build his romantic relationships on his finances and therefore, does not fear the relationship will fail if he encounters financial difficulty
- When it comes to the women he attracts, he believes he is an incredible man with so much to offer, and doesn't ever feel the need to waive his wealth to impress her (nor does he air his finances to impress men)
- He knows he can provide and is comfortable with provision and all things money, even if he is still learning and growing in this area
- He knows that even when he "fails" that he will get back up in no time
- He knows even if he were to lose all his money, he wouldn't lose his identity
- He has such a deep state of inner strength that he knows he can overcome any financial circumstance
- He is ever-evolving and increasing his financial achievements and influence as a direct effect of his personal sense of value
- He understands the balance and correlation of rest and growth
- He is able to be present in his current finances while allowing himself to create his dream financial future

- He challenges himself beyond his comfort zone while maintaining financial stability
- He operates in the balance of risk and security
- He isn't afraid to take risks and isn't reckless in risk-taking
- He knows that he doesn't simply create wealth, but that he IS wealth, abundance, and provision
- He trusts Life
- He trusts Himself
- **He knows and embodies the power of true confidence - the ONE thing needed to attract the woman of his dreams and keep her satisfied**

XXOO

Glory wrapped itself up in one word - you.

- Colette

6

SPIRITUAL

To be spiritual is the most natural expression a man can have, even more so than his desire to prosper, protect, or provide. Yes, even more so than his desire to have mind blowing - and other things blowing - hot AF sex.

Now, I know what you're thinking...but let's just pretend you believe me for a moment.

To be spiritual is natural because you are.

What is not natural (but unfortunately normal) is to be mindfucked, limited, or controlled by any system - religious, societal, familial, or otherwise. And because in a very real sense, we were, more often than not, raised to believe in our limitations rather than our unlimited divinity.

This has heavily influenced our resistance (and rightfully so) to the notion of a God who wants us to obey dutifully and give total control over to Him. Under this belief, if we do this (and do it right), He will take care of us, and if we don't, we're shit out of luck.

Hence we separate our sexuality and other natural ambitions from our spirituality, but **this disintegration was never the optimal human configuration.**

We work best when we feel whole. When we feel fragmented, our energy is divided between various focal points. It is taxing to the system to manage all those variables running at the same time, albeit most are running subconsciously.

Others of us have accepted this notion that God wants to control us, but have made it *okay* because He is "loving" and "because He is, He will make sure everything works out for us in the end," a spiritual life insurance of sorts.

Those who hold to this belief accept that they are spiritual, or believers, but sometimes to the disdain of other natural, beautiful and good human drives. To them, it can be challenging to figure out exactly what God wants from them in order to make Him *happy* and so that, in turn, He will "bless" their lives.

Listen. Spirituality is as natural to the soul as breathing is to the body. It is living in an atmosphere. And the atmosphere where the spirit and soul of a person breathes in true life is the atmosphere of **love**.

God is Love. Period - **end of the BS story.**

And Love is freedom. Total freedom. Love does not want to control, change, or convert. Love simply wants **to know you and to be known by you**. To love God is to love oneself and to love oneself is to love God. And, to love God and oneself is to love others. To the degree that you love yourself, allowing God to love you, is the degree to which you can truly love others. The more you are able to receive love from God, the more you will receive love within yourself and release this love outward. And the more love you receive, the more you are able to give love to those you love. ∞

We will not and cannot receive love from that which we despise, judge, feel unworthy of, or reject. This includes ourselves, God, and others. Nor can we love in that context.

Without love, we lose sight of our heart-centered reasons why, and we invoke alternatives that will lead to our soul's demise. Our heart/soul cannot live without love.

Each area of our life, each expressed state of being, can be driven by love or driven by the want of love. For simplicity sake, let's look at the five main areas within this book. Again they are:

Relationships, Finances, Spirituality/God, Your Physical Being and Sexuality

If your **relationships** are driven by love, they will be full, rich, and joyfully satisfying. You will feel expanded and refreshed by the mutual exchange of love.

If your relationships are driven by the lack of love, by a want for it, they will feel empty, scattered, draining, disheartening, unfulfilling, etc.

If your **finances** are driven by love, your financial endeavors will be deeply meaningful, greatly impactful, and highly influential.

If your finances are driven by a lack of love, a want for it, your finances will feel in vain, will be held tightly, or used strategically as a means to an end.

If your **spirituality** is driven by love, you will engage your divinity with the Divine freely, and you will feel complete wholeness and soul rest. It will also empower you more than anything else to be all that you know yourself to be.

If your spirituality is driven by a want for love, a sense of separation will be the predominant articulation of the sensation that your soul experiences. You will lack clarity and will feel uncertain, perhaps even deserted.

If your **physical** being is driven by love, you will feel perfect as you are, knowing you are good enough right now. You will feel whole, complete, and lacking nothing. You will know you are safe, secure, and succeeding.

If your physical being is driven by a lack of love, a want for it, you will feel separate inside and out. You will feel shame, regret, disappointed in yourself, and what it is to be unwanted for who you truly are.

If your **sexuality** is driven by love, you will be fully present in your sexual encounters, alive in your expression, and deeply in love with your sexual partner. You will be completely confident and passionate in your lovemaking, which allows you to experience new depths of intimacy and more vivid and intense sexual encounters.

If your sexuality is driven by a lack of love, a want for it, you will feel disconnected from the permanency of love. You will feel critiqued, measured, and lacking. You will question your partner, question yourself. You will feel detached from wholeness, a lack of peace, an incomplete sensation, that there is more you cannot seem to experience. You will even feel a sense of being unclean, which is the soul's way of demanding the purest sexual expression.

The soul has high standards.

Love is the driving force that both gives meaning to your life and makes your life meaningful to others. Love connects you to you and you to others. Love solidifies who you are and why you're here. Love answers the questions.

Love questions the answers.

Love establishes a firm foundation for all that you are and all that you do. Love is the cause, and love is the cure.

Therefore, in order to receive love from God or anyone else, you must first be willing. As easy as that sounds, so much subconscious resistance rises up against our willingness. You must also believe you are worthy of love and that the *other* is worthy to give that love to you.

When you see how lovable you are, you become as such. From **that** place, the significant others in your life are then able to see, feel, and experience the love in you for them.

Love is not merely words - it is an **encounter**.
Love is not merely actions - it is an **experience**.
Love is not something someone does or shows -

Love is an extension of who you are.

Love is the presence of the intention of your heart as it speaks to the heart of another. You've certainly experienced the difference between hearing "I love you" from someone who didn't seem to have it and someone else who embodied those words. By "it," I mean the substance to what they said. You can hear, feel, know intimately, and receive love inside of yourself when love is substantiated.

Relationally speaking, you are likely not looking for a mere company of convenience. You are looking to share your life, your very heart and soul with another person, not just your time, bed, or bank account.

One of the greatest hindrances to having the openness such depth requires is the culmination of:

How you feel God feels about you
What you think God thinks of you
What you believe God believes about you

And ultimately, how you perceive God to be *responding* to you because of these aforementioned.

When a man's core belief is I am not enough, he will have many of the following feelings, thoughts, and experiences in his spirituality/his relationship with God:

- Has very mixed feelings about God
- Feels like he is pleasing God one moment, disappointing God the next
- Feels like he is forgiven by God one moment, guilty again in the next
- Feels ashamed for his failings and wonders if God is ashamed of him, too
- Feels fearful; thinks he is going to be punished for his "sins"
- Thinks he can never fully measure up to being the man God wants him to be
- Tries harder to be better
- Hides the behaviors he is ashamed of, justifies them, makes them okay in his mind, but feels deep down that they are the reasons why God is disappointed in him or upset with him

- Thinks his shameful behavior disgusts God and proves that he is unworthy
- Thinks he needs to prove that he is worthy in order to be deserving or accepted by God
- Thinks that since God is "always right," that makes him always *wrong*
- Doesn't trust God
- Feels he has no wiggle room in his relationship with God for a personal view of things
- Thinks God isn't answering his prayers
- Remembers what he has done wrong to deserve his prayers not being answered
- Constantly compares himself to what he should or shouldn't be doing
- Secretly hates that he has to have his behavior monitored and approved of by God
- Hates the feeling of being controlled, watched, or treated like a child
- Has an undercurrent of fear, isolation, or distance
- Feels that he is unloved, not God's pride and joy
- If he attends church, he feels somewhat isolated from other church-going men, like he doesn't really fit in or belong; tries to fit in and be accepted by those who seem to have it all together; fears he won't be
- Avoids church, spiritual gatherings and religious people like the plague; would rather do it alone or figure it out on his own
- Is frustrated with the discrepancies between how he thinks God should be, how others say God is, and how he experiences God to be
- Believes he is ultimately forgiven, but is still somewhat of a disappointment to God
- Fears his ultimate outcome; fears the unknown he is heading towards (the afterlife)

- Thinks if he can **spiritually** please or impress, if God really loves him and if he does the right things, he will attract the woman of his dreams and keep her satisfied

A man who is openly spiritual, but has the core belief **I am not enough** will also believe God agrees (although he may consciously think he thinks otherwise) and is right in determining him to be not good enough. But since he is spiritual (wants a relationship with God), he desires to please God and to be accepted by God. He longs to have a close relationship with his Creator, to know and understand and to be known and understood.

He will try harder, doing things like setting more goals, working to be more disciplined, and focusing on improving his shortcomings. Until he fails at this, which he hopes he won't, but deep down knows he will because he always does.

When he fails, he feels as if God moves away from him, so he moves away into his "corner." This separation, the gap between them, seems to widen with time.

The soul silence increases until it deafens.

He finds himself in the cycle of being closer to God when he is doing or being what he considers to be *good*, and farther away when he is doing or being what he considers to be *bad*. A man in this state will also suffer deep **shame**.

To the contrary, a man who has cut off his spirituality/relationship with God has also cut off certain emotions and sensations. Because of this, he will have familiarity with frustration, anger, a raging sex drive, resentment, and bitterness. A man in this state will also suffer deep **loneliness**.

———

John rode the fence. Part of him wanted to know God, to have a relationship with the One who created him. Part of him wanted nothing to do with God. It wasn't that John was uncertain about what he wanted; he was just uncertain that he could have it in the way he wanted it.

When I asked him what he wanted, he shared freely and without hesitation. He wanted to know that he was, in fact, good enough. That he passed the test.

He wanted to know that his efforts to be a good man, to do right, to succeed at work and in life were noticed and acknowledged. That he wasn't a screwup. That he wasn't falling short. That he wasn't like his *father*.

He also wanted to know that he was safe, meaning that he would go to "Heaven." Although, he openly admitted that he wasn't exactly sure what that place was and that the idea of "singing praises to God for all eternity" sounded borderline with the *other* destination. He wanted to be sure though, sure of his fate.

He was raised Catholic and knew all about Jesus dying for his sins...and that if he received this Jesus "into his heart" that he would be guaranteed to go to Heaven when he died. He shared how he always felt like he was a disappointment to his Catholic parents and grandparents growing up, who wanted him to be a "good boy."

John didn't want to be *good*.

It's not that he wanted to be *bad*, it's just that good didn't appeal to him because it meant tame, governed, subservient. As a boy, he wanted nothing more than to be strong and free. Still does.

So the notion of *this* God left a bad taste in his mouth. He said he did believe there was a God out there somewhere. And that he did want to understand the truth about God and what He thought of him. John would talk to this unknown God sometimes when he needed help and even argue with this invisible Being other times when he was mad as hell at the life he'd been dealt.

When I asked him, "Let's say this **God is your ideal God,** what would this Being be thinking while observing you?"

John quickly responded, "That He's not disappointed in me and never has been. That He loves me...is proud of me. He wouldn't be thinking of how to change me, or make me better, but would be thinking of what He likes about me. He wouldn't be keeping track of my mistakes or waiting for me to blow it again. He would encourage me and be excited to see me growing and changing. Hell, He'd give me credit for trying at least. He would see me as a real man, a good man, a *great* man even."

He managed to laugh as he finished, adding, "Is God even a *He* these days?"

John knew what he wanted in his spirituality. He knew what he wanted to feel about God and about himself. He knew, but he questioned if any of it was real and how he would ultimately know.

A man who has the core belief I AM enough will feel secure in his spiritual relationship with himself and with God, and he will feel, think, and be much of the following:

- He feels FREE
- He knows God trusts him and trusts his choices

- He lives trusting in God, Life, and Himself
- He is at peace; his soul is at rest, unanxious
- He hides nothing from God
- He feels loved, accepted, and wanted
- He knows that God is proud of him
- He feels pride in himself
- He knows he's forgiven and "sin" is a non-issue
- He knows he is allowed to lead his own life
- He feels unlimited and knows he is unlimited
- He knows he has been created on purpose with a purpose
- He knows that he is co-creating his future
- He knows his life's work is worthy and a reflection of his identity
- He knows church attendance is a non-issue and is free from performance and religious penance
- He knows he hears from God and that God hears him
- He feels freedom in his relationship with God to talk openly and speak the truth about what he thinks, what he wants, and how he feels
- He knows and sees what he wants for himself and for his life
- He feels confident that God wants him to have what he wants
- He feels assured that he will get what he wants
- He knows that all of his desires are pure
- He feels powerful, abundant, invincible, unfuckwithable
- **He knows and embodies the power of true confidence - the ONE thing needed to attract the woman of his dreams and keep her satisfied**

xxoo

When we feel out of control in our internal world,

we micromanage our external.

- Colette

7

PHYSICAL

When you are not secure in your **physical enoughness**, it will silently sabotage your view of self and your self-expression, diffusing into your relationships, causing a rift that will eventually cause a split.

A house made of cards always falls.

Now listen. You are rock solid. We just need to clear up some misconceptions that keep you from seeing your brilliance, your attractiveness, and your *machismo*.

Author's Note: The word machismo just popped into my mind, so I used it. But, I actually had to look it up to see what it meant.

Strong or aggressive masculine pride.

The subconscious mind is quite amazing. This is precisely what I want you to have: strong - will stop at nothing to get the breakthrough - masculine pride. The root word *macho* similarly means: aggressively proud of his masculinity. And yes, that is exactly what I want for you - driven by love, of course, knowing who the eff you are, and damn proud of it, too.

When it comes to the physical expression of who you are, it is more than just your appearance or bodily strength. You are a mind, body, heart, and soul - and these coalesce to create the YOU that we see and come to know in the natural.

In this chapter, I will give you a brief overview of the Mind, Soul, and Heart, and will expand and focus more on the Body. Of course, there is so much more to these first areas, but for the sake of the scope and focus of this book, I will keep them short and sweet.

Your **mind** represents your intellect, understanding, knowl-edge-base, perceptions, self-expression, articulation, memory, cognizant creative abilities, and the transference of all of those to the mind of others. The mind is your reflected and perceived self.

The belief **I am not enough** shows up here as thoughts and feelings of not being smart or smart enough to stand out, not understanding things as easily as others, not having a large enough knowledge base, unable to self-express/articulate accurately or effectively, forgetfulness, lack of creative/inno-vative imagination, isolation, or separation from the minds of others...

It causes you to perceive and, therefore, reflect a poor repre-sentation of who you are, and it also prevents you from seeing others for who they are. It's a royal mindfucker.

Your **soul** represents your inward man, your inner BEing, personality, uniqueness, your *true* self. Your soul has senses, eyes/ears, desires, gifts to share, a message to share, presence with substance, wisdom/a knowing. Your soul has a mind of its own. "He" is complete, lacking in nothing.

Your soul fears nothing.

It is, therefore, obvious why the soul is the seat of true confidence, masculinity, and *enoughness*. **Any and all struggle outwardly is a reflection of an inward wrestling with one's soul.**

The belief **I am not enough** shows up here, but not in the soul directly, since this is where your **I AM enough** actually lives. Rather, the belief **I am not enough** will prevent your soul from BEing freely expressed through your heart, mind, and body.

This false belief (appearing real) will cause you to feel as though you are not grand - that you do not have something unique and of great value to share with the world. **I am not enough** creates interference with your soul's truth and causes you to feel a lack of deeply rooted confidence in yourself (identity). Speaking of identity, when it comes to your masculinity, **I am not enough** causes you to perceive other men as being innately more manly than you, which causes you to feel shame or embarrassment…

Your **heart** represents your capacity and depth for love and intimacy. It holds your true and secret desires. It is where you experience love, wholeness, peace, trust, and oneness (BEing one with Self, God, and others). Your heart is the channel, gateway, or portal to the realm of your soul and also to "God." Depending on your perception, you may refer to this as Light, The Universe, Source, etc., but it is essentially the **spiritual dimension**. In this dimension, you are able to encounter the highest vibrations, limitless potential, and all knowledge. Your heart also remembers love and loss, joy and sorrow. It desires to be freed from painful memories and waits for you to release them so it can be free. Your heart has a mind of its own.

The belief that **I am not enough** shows up here as thoughts and feelings of emptiness, darkness, heaviness, separation, anxiety, fear, painfully deep loneliness, isolation, distance, being unwanted, being unloved, needing to tough it out, hopelessness...Or, you may feel nothing at all, a complete disconnection with yourself by way of the heart.

Perhaps you say to yourself, "What's the matter with you!?" Implying that something surely must be. You may even coach yourself to *toughen up, stop being so soft, get over it, get it together*, or as John used to say, *suck it up with a straw.*

Your **body** represents your stature and build, physique and physical attractiveness, stamina and vigor, athleticism and strength, coordination and balance, natural talents and abilities, your health, age, and the age you appear.

It's your hairline, hair color, and thickness, your personal style and attire...everything physical about you - from your teeth right down to your toenails. Your body incorporates it all, yes, even your hand size, shoe size, the size of your genes...You name it. Yes, I know you have a name for it.

Your body in itself is impressive. You can shape and mold it, change and grow it. (I know, some things are harder than others.) It serves you day in and day out, performing the tasks you assign it and most without even needing any instruction. The body has a mind of its own.

I'm sure you can think of things you wished were different about your body. Things you wished you could change. There may even be things you hate about it, or wished to rearrange. Those are especially easy to name because you have long held them against yourself, bearing the guilt and shame.

I was talking to a man the other day. He had a brilliant light, and I was completely drawn to get to know him, even as we stood on the street corner nearing nightfall. He shared his story with passion, how he ended up standing there looking for work.

At one point while he was sharing, he quickly covered his teeth and looked away, meanwhile apologizing for speaking awkwardly to me. I had been so transfixed on who he was in the moment that I hadn't even noticed his teeth, which had apparently been knocked out by a wood plank to the face. He felt so much shame, and I, deep compassion, wanting him to see what I could see and to know that what he covered in shame could never hold a candle to his light.

A man who has the core belief I am not enough will have many of the following feelings, thoughts, and actions regarding his body:

- Tries to hide his flaws
- Is ashamed or embarrassed of himself and works hard to eradicate those embarrassments
- Feels hopeless if he cannot alter them
- Overcompensates in a physical area he knows he can succeed in
- Bases his worthiness, desirability or attractiveness on his physical attributes
- Uses other strong suits like finances or intellect to attract if he feels he isn't able to fully attract stand-alone
- Thinks that the woman he really wants won't want

him until he fixes X, Y, Z; thinks he cannot have her if he cannot fix X, Y, Z

- Thinks about his perceived flaws while interacting with a woman and wonders if she notices them and tries to distract her from them
- Thinks the woman he desires would not find him attractive anymore if she knew his hidden flaws
- Hides behind a physical area that he feels is acceptable in or has achieved success in (physique, athleticism, attire, etc.)
- Thinks he needs to dress to impress; thinks he doesn't know how to dress to impress; thinks he really impresses because of how he dresses
- Worries that aging diminishes his attractiveness
- Thinks he is less manly because of his physical attributes (stature, build, looks, abilities, etc.)
- Thinks he is more manly because of his physical characteristics
- Flaunts his attractiveness because experience has taught him that he wins easily in this area
- Doesn't even try because experience has taught him that he loses when it comes to the physical
- Thinks if he can **physically** please or impress, he will attract the woman of his dreams and keep her satisfied

———

John didn't feel old yet, but he also knew he wasn't young anymore, either. He had reached a sort of middle ground. He knew he was in the gray zone, so to speak. No, I'm not referring to his hair, although he did have more gray these days.

The gray zone I'm referring to is that place where you know

you're not losing entirely, but you're not exactly winning, and you aren't sure you would win outright if you were up against men who were somewhat younger or who had better managed their physique.

John used to have more energy to mess around on the court. He missed being more active. Although he did have a pretty steady gym routine, he felt that it was more basic maintenance status.

He didn't want to be just okay in the physical department. He wanted to knock it out of the park. He wanted to know he still had it. *Game*, that is.

Nicole never said anything about him physically. John said that was part of the problem. She never complimented him, looked at him with longing eyes, or ran her fingers along his chest. She just seemed to avoid physical closeness and touch, or worse, not even notice him.

John wanted her to say something, *anything* to remind him that he still had it. That he was still attractive to her. That he was still a beast.

She didn't. Which he could only assume meant she wasn't turned on or enamored with him or the way he looked anymore.

When John saw himself in the mirror, he was well aware of the change. He knew he didn't look the way he used to, and worried he was losing his edge. He spent less and less time in front of the mirror and would get ready quickly to avoid the whole mirror, mirror on the wall conversation.

John admitted that all this body stuff did have an effect on his sex life. He was definitely distracted when he tried to turn Nicole on. He wasn't sure he could draw her in with his body anymore, so he studied techniques that were supposed to "get her in the mood." Take the focus off of him, put the focus on her. (More on that in the next chapter.)

When a man doesn't feel good about the way he looks, he often has cyclical sub/conscious thoughts.

I don't like the way I look. (Feels bad.) I want to be happy with the way I look. I need to look a certain way so I can feel good about myself, then I'll be happy with how I look. If I achieve looking that way, I will feel really good. I'll finally get admiration, attention, sex, love, etc. I will fix this.

If he fixes it, he then gives himself permission (subconsciously) to believe that he is "attractive." If he couldn't fix it, he reminds himself that he is still not attractive, followed by: *I don't like the way I look. Feels bad.* Said cycle repeats...

When you don't think you are good enough, you will simultaneously believe that you are not worthy of what you desire. When you do something to make yourself "good enough," you now think that you are.

The "good enough" shift isn't in your appearance, it's in your **belief** that you now *are*. This is to put the horse before the cart. In essence, you "earned" the right to be good enough for or worthy of what you want. However, all that was actually needed all along was **to believe that you already are.**

To decide it.

For the man with the core belief **I am not enough**, this habit of convincing himself that he is now (fill in the blank) because of what he has done does work, but only temporarily because his core operating belief will always rise up in resistance.

This idea of earning our identity or value physically is evident in advertising and marketing strategies, which are directed to those who don't feel good enough about themselves.

Buy this and you will finally be good enough...Still not good enough? Oh, that's because you also need this and this and that...We have just the right product or service for you!!

When it comes to the physical body, a man with the core belief I AM enough will think, feel, and demonstrate the following:

- He's comfortable with his body - imperfections and all
- He strengthens and moves his body regularly because it feels good to do so
- He works with his body while knowing he can and will perform, not *against* it (driving it harshly towards an intended goal)
- He knows he is attractive and feels no shame
- He knows he increases in attractiveness and magnetic masculinity with age because it's a byproduct of increasing his connectedness to his inner flow of confidence
- He is impressed with himself, proud of who he is and how he shows up in life
- He does not feel the need or desire to physically impress others
- He is full of hope and excitement for what is coming to him, regardless of his age or stage in life
- He neither hides nor flaunts his attractiveness; **he embodies it and owns it**
- He knows he is a real man's man
- He doesn't hide who he *really* is

- He enjoys who he is and enjoys life
- He is rested (not anxious) in his nature and at rest in his body
- He has enhanced vigor and feels refreshed, like he caught his second wind in life
- He is inspired, intuitive, and creative
- He has a flow of innovative thoughts and ideas
- He increases in wisdom and understanding
- His memory improves as his insecurity lessens
- He is naturally followed by others who want to know what he has and how he does what he does
- He knows there is nothing to fix about himself because there is nothing broken
- He understands how to connect to his innate masculine flow and move through life from that energy source
- He increases in his capacity to love and receive love
- He navigates his emotions with ease and stride
- He stabilizes - feels more and more in control and less and less out of control
- He significantly increases his mental and physical energy because he is centered
- He no longer feels scatterbrained due to anxiety, stress, insecurity, worry, or fear
- He knows he is worthy of the woman of his dreams and attractive enough for her
- **He knows and embodies the power of true confidence - the ONE thing needed to attract the woman of his dreams and keep her satisfied**

xxoo

The problems in your sex life have never been about sex.

- Colette

8

SEXUAL

John cried himself to sleep last night.

He barely admitted it to me and the shame of it was written all over his face when he did. He had worked with me long enough by this point to know that I am a safe place in which to share anything.

"I'm so hurt. I feel RAW these days. This opening my heart shit has really opened me up to a lot of pain."

I know, love.

Pain isn't something that comes upon you when you open your heart, although it can feel that way. It comes from within you, yes. BUT, it is actually trying to make its way out of you, so let it.

It takes a lot of energy to keep pain hidden away, numbed out, and stuffed down. But once you actually face it and move through it, there is a real releasing of it. This release causes incredible joy, freedom, and expansion. Not to mention it frees up a LOT of energy! I'm sure you could think of a few things you'd like to do with all that energy - *one* in particular sounds incredible right about now. This is the sex chapter, after all...

John wasn't entirely convinced, but he had seen enough results to trust the process. The "process" I'm referring to is not something dry, rigid, or systematic. In fact, it's not even linear. The process of transformation involves a much more intricate system with an immeasurably higher processing center - your soul. He knows everything about you, and this includes exactly what needs to come up and when. He knows precisely how you will shift from **I am not enough** to **I AM enough**, and He intimately knows how you will draw in the woman you are desiring. John decided to trust the process (a very powerful decision).

We talked about what was coming up for him, what was **beneath the hurt**. There is ALWAYS a message trying to come through. Of course, it is always about you.

Depending on your current level of self-awareness and healing, the message coming through is often **not** a true statement of your identity, and in which case, needs to be removed. Or rather, **re-truthed**.

When it came to sex, John wasn't "good enough," or so he thought. It was obvious Nicole didn't find him sexually desirable anymore. She seemed to have lost all interest. Never initiated. Stopped showing any affection, inside and outside the bedroom.

Nicole spent her time doing things for herself or by herself. She even seemed annoyed when spending time with John, as if she would rather be doing something else altogether.

How did it get so bad?

How did I go so wrong?

And why does it always seem to go this way?

Why do things just end up dying out? I don't understand!

Babe, listen to me. You ARE the mother fucking shit - a badass in business and in bed. But you have for damn sure forgotten.

It is up to YOU to remember who you are.

No one will do that for you, and no one can, for that matter. You can listen to positive thinking meditations, motivational speakers, mindset reset coaches, whatever the fuck. I don't care what it is - **IF YOU DON'T RELEASE THE INNER RESISTANCE AND OWN THE FUCK OUT OF WHO YOU ARE, you will NEVER get there**. And by "there," I mean to your real identity, to knowing fully who you are, to walking in true confidence, and to living empowered in your own masculine essence - the expression of which is **unique to you**.

Have you ever tapped into your own source? Have you ever experienced this unstoppable force of identity and confidence? Have you lost touch with the confidence that once flowed so easily and effortlessly through you? If you've had even a taste of this, can you remember it, how you felt? Do you remember how easy it was to attract women, business opportunities, pretty much whatever you wanted?

And now? Whether you have had a taste of your own glory or if you've never tasted and seen, confidence always - 100% of the time - without exception, affects your sexual experience and expression.

You may or may not initially see that, especially if you have perfected your performance and "have never had any issues bringing a woman to climax." But the truth is, if you don't know who the fuck you are, then you are not connected with your soul. Your soul is the ultimate Source of **I AM enough**. He *owns* that wholly. He has zero doubts about himself and not a single cell of insecurity.

Do you understand that when you coalesce (align, unify, connect) with Him, the YOU that you become doesn't merely have confidence? **HE IS CONFIDENCE**. And do you know that if you are not unified within yourself, then you cannot connect to your sexual partner in any way beyond the mere physical aspects of sex?

If you want to go beast-mode in your sexuality, you have to play in the big leagues, baby. And if all you know is the physical shit, you are still playing the amateur.

Women who are more advanced in their evolution of soul will also likely have more exceptional experiences and sensations when it comes to sexual pleasure. They have played on the adult playground of **multidimensional sex**. And once you play there, the mere physical can no longer satisfy your sexual-spiritual appetite and craving.

Now, you don't have to have sex with this kind of woman, but your soul-Self reeeeaaaallly likes it, so I highly recommend you grasp and pursue this.

Remember how I told you that you only attract according to what you **are**, not merely what you desire? That you cannot attract what you haven't attained and that you only attract on your level? I'm talking *energetics*, not economics.

How's that been working out for you?

If you are desiring the woman of your **dreams**, she isn't average. This means you can't be either.

Now, maybe you are well-endowed, fully equipped, extensively experienced, and wildly expressive. Perhaps you know all the right ways of getting your partner to come with you on a magic carpet ride into a whole new world of orgasmic euphoric fuck-me-now bliss. Maybe your sexual performance is your strong suit. Perhaps sex is where you assume *I've got this*.

Well, if you aren't embodying **I AM enough**, then even with all of the above, you don't. You've just learned how to get really good at performing a function of your human body.

Sex is more than sex. Sex is doorway into a dimension of exploration and experience, unlike ANYTHING else this world offers. But if you only perform physically, even if you outperform 100% of all other men in this area, you are banging up against a locked door. And why on earth would you do that, when you could enter it and find out what mind-blowing pleasures sex really has to offer on the other side?!

When you understand and experience this, you also find places where you can take your partner. Honey, you can show her things no other man can. I say *no other man* because what you have is unique to you - but you don't actually *have* it unless you've **accessed** it.

Allow me to exemplify. If you have a bank account with an enormous amount of money in it but have no way to make a withdrawal, you would have it, but not *have* it. In sex, if you haven't accessed the soul realm, you "have it" by design, but don't have it by experience.

And you CANNOT give what you do not have (energetic

principals will always override the physical). If you want to be able to give your sexual partner more than the average man, you have to rise above the norm of offering a mere physical experience. So as I was saying...

Honey, you can show her things no other man can. You can take her places no other man can. You can give her experiences no other man can. But you can't do any of this if you don't lead her through the door between the worlds.

You possess the golden key, so take that key and open the damn door.

By the way, a woman who knows this place for herself has something she can show you that the average woman cannot. She can take you places the average woman cannot. And she can give you experiences the average woman cannot.

This type of woman has a honey pot of sticky sweet nectar that both satisfies and awakens desire. It heals and reveals. It expounds and expands. There is nothing like it on this planet. No mere physically sexual encounter will ever compare to the experience of sex with a woman embodying her soul and deeply present to you.

She will open another warm, wet place for you to enter and explore even while your bodies intertwine. Sexual experiences of this kind allow you the adventure of truly being *known* and that of *knowing* - all of which cannot be contained in words or comprehended with the mind. But, please allow your imagination to run away with your pants on this one.

Now, when a man doesn't embody the identity of **I AM enough**, it will affect his sexuality and his sexual expression. If he continues to suffer from this insecurity, it will take a major toll on him.

He will begin to experience some of the following:

- Performance anxiety
- Sexual addictions
- Erectile Dysfunction
- Trying harder (if he could just do better)
- Overthinking
- Way overthinking
- Trying to give her "the best" and multiple orgasms
- So much trying
- Over-studying how to excite the female body
- Way over-studying
- Over-studying how to fix his sexual concerns
- Way over-studying
- Reading too many damn emails and articles on testosterone and men's hormones
- Chasing more and more testosterone
- Racing thoughts
- Distracted thoughts
- Dark thoughts
- Guilty Thoughts
- Shameful thoughts
- Thoughts of other women...a lot of them

If you are familiar with these, then you know how fucking exhausting and often overwhelming they can be. You may even think it's hopeless.

When a man's core operating belief is I am not enough, he will experience many of the following thoughts, feelings, and behaviors when it comes to his sexuality, performance, and expression:

- Struggles with performance anxiety and pre-performance anxiety
- Thinks way too much about performing
- Isn't able to perform the way he wants, which will cause him to have even more anxious thoughts
- Wonders if she is pleased with him
- Looks for *physical* clues that she is enjoying the sex, that he is doing a good job (some women will fake this)
- Will have anxious thoughts if he thinks she is not
- Thinks of what to do to ensure she is pleased
- Tries harder
- Gets frustrated with himself
- Gets frustrated with her
- Expects her to initiate, perform, please him, meet his sexual needs; thinks other women do, so why doesn't she
- Over-studies how to please a female body
- Doesn't know how to really connect to her, read body and her energetic cues
- Has racing thoughts
- Has distracting thoughts
- Feels shame
- Tries to blackout sexual memories that trigger the shame
- Longs to be accepted sexually even in his current sexual state
- Fears starting a new relationship because she will find out his sexual shortcomings
- Fears she will reject him for not being enough sexually
- Constantly wonders if she is happy with him
- Suffers from not being able to climax or climaxes too quickly

- Frequently second-guesses himself
- Doesn't know how to get out of his head and sexually lead with his heart and soul
- Recalls the time(s) when he felt sexually powerful; longs to go back to "her" or get back to that version of himself
- Struggles with sexual confusion and dark fantasies
- Is overtaken by sexual desires and doesn't know how to manage his sexual energy
- Struggles connecting to women on a heart level
- Thinks if anyone knew these things about him, he would be exposed as not being a real man
- Thinks other men are better than him in the sexual arena
- Secretly believes the woman he is with (or could potentially be with) would be happier with another man
- Has sex addictions, porn, constant masturbation, multiple partners, one night stands
- Struggles with feeling truly lovable
- Thinks sexually pleasing = pleasing a woman
- Thinks if he can **sexually** please or impress, he will attract the woman of his dreams and keep her satisfied

When you are operating from **I am not enough**, it WILL affect your sexuality and relational intimacy, silently sabotaging your sexual experience and diffusing into every area of the relationship.

This is why your relationships end.
This is why they die out.
Because YOU do.

When a man has the core belief **I AM enough**, his sexual experience dramatically transforms.

The sexual beast emerges in glory.

He c.o.m.e.s.ALIVE.

He sheds the weight of the world.

He feels like he rose from the dead.

He's faced the inner struggle and won.

When a man's core operating belief is I AM enough, he will experience many of the following thoughts, feelings, and behaviors about his sexuality, performance, and expression:

- He knows how to feast on his masculine glory
- He shows up to the sexual encounter full from within, ready to give and to receive
- He enjoys himself through and through
- He knows that he is utterly desirable and completely satisfying
- He easily and effortlessly connects to a woman sexually
- He is proud of himself and of how he shows up to life as a sexual being
- He understands how to move into her energy
- He feels her engaging him with her heart, soul, mind, and body
- He penetrates her deeply and thoroughly - I'm talking all the way to HER
- He knows how to fill her wholly with his presence
- He magnetizes and captivates
- He confidently approaches sex, knowing his body serves his desires

- He isn't thinking with either head during sex because he knows how to confidently move with the energy of his being
- He moves in the flow of his innate masculine sexuality - a powerfully driven inner guide that takes both him and his sexual partner on the ride of their lives
- He loves himself and knows how to make love within himself, rather than merely "let off steam" (Masturbation 2.0)
- He has total control of his sexual energy and directs it on purpose
- He has no sexual confusion
- He has no self-doubt
- He knows he is the best she has ever had
- He doesn't struggle with comparison
- He feels no shame
- He trusts himself
- He feels wild, adventurous, and free
- He sees the sexual encounter as his playground, his open field, his table of delights
- He knows he is a safe place for a woman to open up fully - body, heart, and soul
- He knows how to select a sexual partner with whom he can open up fully - body, heart, and soul, and in whom he can genuinely enter and rest
- He makes love with an open heart and knows loving making comes from the heart
- He experiences sex the way he desires: connected, deeply satisfying, a full body-soul encounter
- He knows how to deal with any intrusive thoughts or feelings
- He knows how to shift back into confidence easily and at any moment

- He treats himself like a king, with honor and dignity
- He owns the fuck out of his sexuality
- **He knows and embodies the power of true confidence - the ONE thing needed to attract the woman of his dreams and keep her satisfied**

XXOO

A LOVER'S POEM

I give you my life.
I lay myself down.
Even this bed of roses, can't handle the sound.
I don your head with my very own crown.

O lover, love on.
Keep on loving beyond the breaking of dawn.
Your soul is a river my soul knows well.
Our love is a secret I love to tell.

I'm swept by your current.
I drown in your deep.
I come to full consciousness,
Even while we sleep.

You're wide open spaces,
I love to explore.
I'm tightly hidden places.
Your mystery, all the more.

9

SUMMARY

So whatever happened to John?

John got that beautiful gift: clarity. You know, that *Aha!* moment when everything's "*Oooh!*" It was as if his whole life made sense in an instant. He finally saw what he needed to see - that his belief in himself, his worth, his ability (or lack thereof) was the driving force behind all of his choices, and that those choices were causing him to "end up" in the frustrating and disappointing patterns that he was experiencing - *on repeat*. John also saw that these relational patterns directly affected his business endeavors. He wasn't even expecting *that* bonus revelation.

We spoke about connecting to soul, moving through life from his innate masculine flow, and allowing this to create his true desired outcomes in life.

We talked about forgiveness, healing, and restoration, about embodying true confidence, and owning his identity in life. We talked about what he really wanted and how to really get it. And we basked in his glory.

He's pretty happy these days, if you ask me.

So what about you?

Are you ready to live knowing you are enough?

Do you want to finally BE who you really are?

Do you want to finally understand and embody true confidence?

Do you want to finally walk in the energy that attracts the woman of your dreams?

Are you ready to finally own the fuck out of life in all areas?

This book was designed to give you perspective. It was written to reveal to you what's been holding you back. And I didn't hide the answers on how to get it, either. But, I'm no fool. I know the hardest part isn't taking action - you're really good at that.

The hardest part is **believing**.

It seems so simple, and it IS simple. But, it does require **shifting the internal shit that keeps you from believing** in your incredible greatness and keeps you stuck in belief cycles of a lesser version of yourself.

As you were reading this book and seeing what it's like when a man walks in **true identity and confidence**, did you ever wonder if after a man figures out this whole identity and confidence business if he just gets it from then on out? Did it raise questions like: Does he never feel insecure or fearful again? Does he never have self-doubt after that? Is he supposed to be like a superhuman all the time?

If you had thoughts along those lines, you are on to something, and here's the truth of the matter: You are a perfect Soul having an imperfect human experience. Sometimes you are connected and flowing, and sometimes life sidetracks you, triggering you to disconnect from the power source of **I AM enough**.

Guess what? That's a normal part of the process. As you work through the limiting beliefs, internal resistance, facing your fears head on, you will experience growth. You were meant to overcome.

Growth involves getting better and faster at recognizing the BS BS (bullshit belief systems). It means an increased awareness (sensitivity) to your thoughts and feelings, which is essential to monitoring your state of BEing. You will also improve your assessment of what's really going on in you and what roots you're dealing with when things come up for you. And they do come up *for* you.

Every time you are ready to go to the next level, or even take a quantum leap over multiple levels of growth all at once, you will have certain experiences in the transitional period. Instantaneous and easy shifts **do** occur and ought to be your expectation. However, if you experience any of the following, it is a normal part of the process and doesn't indicate that something is wrong with you.

Discomfort - you are moving out of your comfort zone.

Pain - you are releasing another pocket of pain that you've held onto. (BS beliefs are tied to a memory with an attached emotion that you have been avoiding.)

Fear - you are moving away from the known into the unknown, and this can feel scary because you temporarily lose your footing as your previous ceiling becomes your new floor.

Awareness of an area of separation or disintegration from your soul (ex. insecurity, guilt, shame) - it's coming up for you to shift a BS BS and release yourself from the false identity associated with it.

This awareness, although really good, can sometimes feel really shitty. But it passes quickly if you relax (don't resist) and go with the flow. Much like the process of passing the *other* shitty shit.

If you stay grounded and connected to your soul, you'll move through this transition, releasing what needs to be released so that your now freed-up energy can empower you in your new level of personal authority and self-expression.

You can do all this processing on your own. You don't need me or anyone else to "help" you. But why would you want to go through it alone? With the right person, it is often easier and faster. When you invite the right person, and by *right*, I mean, the one you feel you can safely expose your shit to and who is wise and experienced in working with innards. *Your* right person can make the process so much more enjoyable, hopeful, and encouraging.

Why would you pay with your money, your time, and your energy to work with someone on your most personal and private matters if you *didn't* think they were right for you?!

So here's the deal. If you like my personality and my take on life and relationships and think it would be amazing to work with me, I would be honored to share my heart, perspective, expert wisdom, and advice with you. I offer Private Coaching so that you can partner with me in your process of exposing the Bullshit Belief Systems (BS BS) and Shifting the

Shit (limitations) that has held you back. I'm really good at this.

I know confidence like the back of my hand.

I eat, sleep, breathe, live it. It's who I AM. It's what I do.

And I know how to unearth it in you. I can guide you to it, and when it clicks for you, it will flow through you with effortless power. When you learn to embody your true confidence, you become a magnetic force of attraction for the woman you desire - and a whole lot of others who just can't take their eyes off you, who just want to be around you, be in your energy. This won't intimidate you or puff you up with pride. **It's just who you are now.**

What's more, when you embody your true confidence, it attracts more than just women. Your magnetic confidence will call in business opportunities in the exact same way, and whatever else you desire.

But honestly, the best part of connecting back to your soul, the seat of confidence, is the peace, fulfillment, and assurance that **you are the man you desire to be**.

You want it? **Come and get it**.

10

RESOURCES

I see you. Your experience here on earth matters to me. I exhort you to your higher potential, and it would be my honor to walk with you on your journey. **It is fully your life to own and entirely your decision to make.**

Wouldn't it be amazing if you could live the best possible version of your life, even if you think you got a late start on it?

Whether we meet in person, by phone, or energetically through my teachings, online courses, audios, and other materials, I look forward to knowing you and to *you* knowing you - fully, even as you are fully known.

Because I love you.

PRIVATE CONSULTING / CONFIDENCE COACHING

I offer Private Consulting and Embodiment Coaching in identity, confidence, sexuality, and relationships (intimacy), especially for men like you.

Why men and why these areas?

Men because I love them! I have a fire in me to see you come alive like never before and to live fully in your God-given identity, masculinity, personal authority, and power.

Confidence because it directly affects every area of your life. I believe confidence is key to personal success and fulfillment in your relationships. Confidence directly influences every aspect of how, when, and why you relate the way you do in all areas of life.

Relationships because I believe we are in relationship with (relating to) everything and everyone around us – all directly mirroring our relationship to our Self. This is without exception.

Sexuality because I like the *hard* topics and because sexuality is central to our humanity. It is an area often misunderstood, misrepresented, and in desperate need of a revolution. I am unafraid and unashamed to talk openly about what happens behind closed doors and what comes out of our bedroom closets.

So tell me, love...

Do you feel stuck or disconnected?

Are your relationships confusing, overwhelming, or empty?

Are you frustrated with feeling uncertain and unfulfilled?

Do you want to overcome insecurities, self-doubt, and fear?

Do you desire to finally feel confident, but don't see what you're missing?

Do you know what's missing and can't seem to fix it?

Are you tired of feeling held back from the life you know you were made for?

My intention with one on one clients is to facilitate the process of personal fulfillment and transformation through identifying and shifting internal resistance to embodying true confidence and experiencing fulfillment, success, and love.

My passion is to work with you to unveil the Man within the man (to the man) and to facilitate this deep inner connection with your truest Self, in order that *He* may reveal himself to you, as you.

I believe our relationship to Self is primary. This belief is central to my transformational and integrative Consulting/Coaching. I work on the basis of individual change begets change in all other aspects.

When you connect deeply to the truth of who you are and remember how to live from this internal Source of self-knowing (identity) and limitless potential (possibility), you will emerge confident like never before. This process leads to breakthroughs in your emotional, relational, and spiritual life. This naturally inspires and renews your physical experience of life, including your body, relationships, and business endeavors.

Breakthrough is YOU breaking through.

The men I work with desire to experience:

- Restored confidence in their personal and romantic relationships
- Increased satisfaction intimately and relationally speaking
- Restored sense of power and personal authority in their business relationships and creative endeavors
- Full confidence as a manifestation of their inner wholeness and connection to personal identity

Regardless of what area is drawing you, you want *clarity*. We all want and need clarity to live powerful and fulfilled lives. When you are clear, you can take decisive action. When you have clarity, you know **who you are, what you want, what has kept you from it, and how to overcome the resistance** - so you can **be** what you need to **be** in order to **have** what you want to **have**. You can learn to design and magnetize the life of your dreams.

Speaking of clarity, details about working with me one on one can be found here:

www.colettelamuse.com/privateconsultingformen

For other offers and resources for men, please visit:

www.colettelamuse.com/for-men

ABOUT THE AUTHOR

Hello love.

I am *The Master and The Muse* of my own life and the Founder of **Colette LaMuse**, a company whose purpose is to inspire, educate, and liberate.

My passion is to inspire others to Self-Mastery through a deep understanding of identity and confidence. From that place, we are able to share our greatest contributions and to live our best lives.

My intention is that you would come to honestly know yourself, be freed from limitations and expectations, boldly and confidently display your magnificence and share your gifts with the world – that you would be confident, happy, powerful, and free.

When you connect to YOU, *that* you has all the confidence, motivation, inspiration, passion, courage, guidance, and wisdom that you need to fulfill why you came to this planet.

As for me, I am most on fire when I teach others how to move from insecurity to confidence, from fear to boldness, from separation to connection, from loneliness to love, and ultimately to fulfillment and freedom.

My work centers around facilitating the dynamic process of inner healing, freedom, and total identity transformation.

Some of my favorite topics are confidence, relationships, and sexuality. But, as you may already know, I have a lot to say about many things.

I am honored to be able to share with men like you through private consulting and confidence embodiment coaching, books, online courses and teachings, and group engagement.

You can connect with me here:

www.colettelamuse.com
facebook.com/colettelamuse
instagram.com/colettelamuse/

HEY HANDSOME.

If you read all the way to this page, consider this a kiss on your forehead.

I want you to know that you are enough, not just for the woman of your dreams, but for everything you dream of. My prayer for you is that you will see who you truly are because that light outshines the stars in the sky. You were made on purpose with a purpose, and this is the time for you to know it.

May you go farther, run faster, dream bigger, live a little wilder, and forever be *free*. And may you know the love that passes knowledge. I am so very proud of you!

You are in my heart.

Always,

Colette

Made in the USA
Monee, IL
09 July 2020

36210940R10066